McAlmon's Chinese Opera

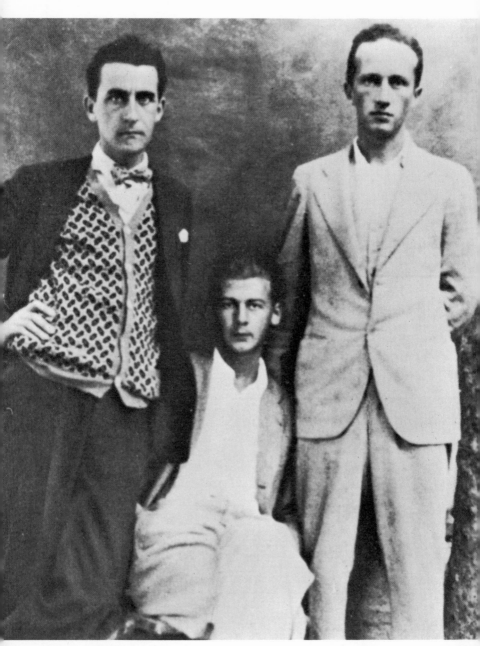

McALMON, GLASSCO AND TAYLOR

McALMON'S CHINESE OPERA

POEMS BY STEPHEN SCOBIE

QUADRANT EDITIONS

Published by Quadrant Editions, RR1 Dunvegan, Ontario K0C 1J0.
Distribution c/o English Department, Concordia University, 1455 de
Maisonneuve Blvd. West, Montreal, Quebec H3G 1M8.

Designed by Tim Inkster, typeset in Syntax by the Coach House Press
(Toronto), printed and bound by the Porcupine's Quill (Erin) in December
of 1980. The stock is Zephyr Antique Laid.

Published with assistance from The Canada Council, The Bronfman
Foundation, and a host of generous subscribers.

Cover is after an etching by Hugh Mackenzie.

ISBN 0-86495-004-7

for Maureen
as always,
          as everything

and also
in gratitude and deep admiration
for John Glassco

I AMERICA (1896-1921)

When I had gone back to the bar to sit with McAlmon again, what happened then was in a sense a parable acted out for exactly what this man was. He had switched from gin to scotch, and we were sitting there silenced and saddened and embittered by the ugliness and the opulence of the middle-aged people, French and American and English, who danced, and ate, and drank, and threw their money away in handfuls instead of giving it to the poets and the beggars of the world. And then, between the silk draperies that completely concealed a window that stood open on the summer night (they were green, those curtains; I can see them clearly, stirring, wavering a little in the night air), suddenly a miserable hand reached in from the deserted street, a black-nailed, dirty, defeated hand, with a foul bit of coat sleeve showing at the wrist. Without a word McAlmon placed his fine, tall glass of whisky and soda into the fingers of the stranger's hand, and the fingers closed quickly on it and drew it back through the draperies into the lonely dark.

Kay Boyle

What I never wanted
was pity
            — like when I posed
as a model in New York,
I could hold positions longer
than any of the others. It
should never have occurred
to anyone to say 'Why don't you
take a rest?' If I had wanted
I'd have walked out soon enough,
for all their flabby drawings made
of how I looked back then.

I mean, no doctor has to tell me
of how a woman tore me up
leaving me cold and rotten inside
like frozen fruit. He doesn't need
to write that shit for all his
drooling public. It
should never have occurred.

I wanted them to draw me as I was:
the line straight and hard,
the muscles firm, not tired at all
nine hours a day
at a dollar an hour
in 1921.

7

You can sit where you like:
the chairs are all the same.
I've never been to Canada.

My mother was born there, she
never talked about it. All
she ever saw was space.
What she wanted was small
kitchens, in smaller houses.
She never lifted her eyes
higher than horizons. She never
travelled further than she needed.
She stuck in one place, and me —
at last I came back to her.
Ten years now I've been in this room,
there's no place else I'll be going.

The chairs are all the same.

Hemingway will tell you stories
about sweet sensitive boys
discovering death
in inarticulate gulps. As for me
I always talked in paragraphs.
It's my impression
I had friends at age eleven
who always finished their sentences
and knew about death.

There was no revelation.
I can't remember a day when it
struck me out of the sky, when I knew
some dead pet pigeon
would never come back, or
garbage like that.

One time in a train at the border
just going into Spain
he wanted me — that's Hemingway —
he wanted me to look
at a dead dog lying by the track.
Various things had been already
eating it. I said I'd rather
go for a drink. He told me I was
avoiding reality, or some such
bull. He sat and studied it
for as long as suited his
heroism. Then came to the bar himself
and talked about it.
                    As for me
I'd seen enough corpses already
floating the Hudson River,
and not dogs either.

(Oh you know that story do you?
I guess I've told it before.)

My father was a nomad pastor,
wandered the Mid-West plains
with the Word in a battered suitcase.
He'd come home with the dust of a dozen states
lined in his face. He was always tired.

He would fly into rages, suddenly, a black
tornado against the livid horizon
collapsing just as suddenly —

then sit in the bathtub and pray
while my mother scrubbed off
the dirt of his travels, and all his children
were banished outside
so we never saw him naked
or clean.

Before he died he went senile
sitting for hours with that suitcase
clutched on his knees,
looking inside it every half hour
and always finding it empty.

10

America we knew was the twentieth century:
no place else was big enough.
I used to walk for days along
roads that cars were just beginning
to make sense of.
                    That was the scale,
and the only possible speed.

Gertrude Stein says
you have to have flown across the Mid-West
seeing the patterns of the fields
to understand modern painting.
What I say is
you have to have walked that land
a whole Dakota afternoon
to understand modern writing.

11

Words fail me
now, in the desert years –
nothing accomplished, contact lost,
they sift across my pages
in meaningless whispers of sand.

When I was young
the only problem was turning
the pages quickly enough – no time
for style or revisions – they came
tumbling through me like rockslides,
direct and indiscriminate:

those fighting words
I shouted across the continent
trying to fill the sky with sound –
they fail me now, they are sand
and whispers, old excuses,
muttered sad apologies.

12

The summer I started travelling:
on the docks at Duluth for three days looking
for jobs on the Great Lakes steel-boats
to take me east to Chicago, and then
who knows how much farther?
But not that year: no jobs, no money,
three days without food, I started walking
back home to Minneapolis, one hundred
and fifty miles, living on handouts
from farmers' wives to whom I pretended
the jaunt was only a college bet.

Got home for supper and left the next day

back to old haunts in South Dakota,
signed on for jobs in harvesting;
hung round the pool-hall, talked with old friends
the speculations of sex, then at night the hunger
alone in bed, or out under the stars
walking till almost dawn. Until

my first girl lay beneath the moon
in an open field on a harvest night.
It was nothing so special, I told myself
and her. She agreed with a smile
I've searched for every since.

13

What I learned on the road
in a half dozen summers:
how to sit for hours not thinking,
how to talk to anyone beside me,
how to drink fast and
                        how to drink slow.

People I met in bars and railroads
travelling west for the time of year:
drunks and hoboes discussing Nietzsche,
teaching me all I know about hope
which extends to only some food, a mattress,
and the time of year for travelling east.

Nights I spent camped out with nothing
except the night itself to talk to,
debating the serious question of whether
it might have been better not to be born:
rolled in a blanket on stony ground,
or sitting on a lakeshore watching stars
drown in their own abstract reflections.

Each winter I went back to school
to learn and forget a few things more
of what some wise men thought good reasons
to get them through till dawn.

14

The pride of my college days is the paper
I wrote proving fifty
great writers and thinkers were all
agnostic or atheist.

The hall of learning was a wooden shack
which acted like an oven in the sun
of South California afternoons –

though it wasn't the heat that caused
my distinguished professor to break out in sweat
as I read through the names.

One student walked out, her pinched pale face
trembling with righteous shock;
my cordial fraternity attempted
to have me expelled for heresy.

I left soon after for Chicago
where the smell of blood
hung in the city's air like honesty.

15

I am watching
my face in the mirror
make its slow changes
nervously, under inspection
of eyes that yield nothing
to weakness or time.

The nose is long
like a bridge across
not a river but a bay;
the clipped moustache
attempts to disguise
the wide and angry mouth
closed like a strongroom door.

The longer I watch
the more the face breaks down;
twenty-four years in America
have not yet fixed it in any
position of comfort; the skin
is constantly twitching, seized
by a frantic dance of deceptions.

Only the mirror on the wall
remains unchanging
all my life, all my long life.

16

Carnevali / God with us:

it seemed we only met in hospitals.
His life was rage
imprisoned by disease. In Chicago
I sat by his bed and listened to
his pure voice blasphemies,
flames locked in ice,
drilling into my head
like a thin perfect wound.

I have never shed a tear for him.
Years later in Italy
I gave him money
and wiped the flies away from his face.

17

Marsden Hartley was the first
and finest of painters I met in New York:
he watched me pose with a lecherous eye
then covered my hand in kisses, bowed,
but otherwise remained discreet. I saw him
two years later in Berlin, surrounded
by throngs of lovely boys, his hair
set into waves, his eyebrows plucked,
a daily orchid in his coat lapel.
Dreams that had been his torment for years
were available cheap, and nothing was left him
but to follow them through to despair.

When I heard he was dead, twenty years later,
I wished I had given him more
of myself, my body, whatever
would for a moment have brought some peace
to his restless soul —

No matter, he's dead
and that's an end to it.
Some cynic called him once
'eagle without a cliff,' but
aren't we all?

New York New York:

I lived above an open sewer the river
and watched it float out to sea
bodies of dogs and Negroes bloated,
decomposing outward from their wounds
frayed ropes like fashionable scarves
looped round their necks and ankles.

Liberty received them all, they
drifted ashore on Ellis Island. Give me
your starving and your poor
your homeless —

          On West 14th Street
I attended the literary parties:
earnest poets deplored the times
and wished for social improvement.
Bill Williams worked twelve hours a day
reclaiming the ones who hadn't made it
as far as the river. I drank
tea from their china balanced cups, and then
stopped in at some speakeasy dive
for a dozen beers before I went home

to my garbage scow on the Hudson River.

19

Tell me what friendship is, does
anyone know? You'll find
another bottle in the bookshelf there
propping up
some priceless first editions of
nobody's autobiography.

I could listen to anyone talk,
I would take what they gave me without
suspicion. But after thirty years
— Christ, you would think you would know
all the damned machinery, head
heart and balls — after
thirty years it hurts like hell
to find there's nothing there at all.

20

I'd meet Bill Williams at the hospital
and prop him up as we walked, he was
so damn tired. We used to sit
on the East River docks, looking over to Brooklyn,
the hollow dirty canyons of Manhattan
behind our backs. We preferred it there —
the river stank with garbage, but at least
it kept on moving. So the tiredness would pass
and he'd begin to recite me his poems,
those images drawn with a doctor's precision
out of the quiet inner country
his eye inhabited. And stories I'd started
during the rigid hours of posing
replied to his poems, made for us both
a dialogue. We sat there for hours

for thirty years we sat there:
at our backs the ravenous city
at our feet the stinking river
and only words to hold us together
against the deaths we dreamed.

21

CONTACT
must be with
everything.

So one day Bill took me along
to meet H.D. And there
was Bryher. It was hard at first
to notice her: an attendant priestess
she waited in shadows, made small
important movements, and only
slowly emerged: the dark
bright eyes intense in her thin
skeleton face, her hair
a fuzz of electric tension. Then
for me she had taken over
that room: from the start I was lost
in all the elaborate lies
we devised from each other's deceptions.

22

At first like a leg-cramp, urgent
pulling me out of sleep with
every nerve screaming;
then like a rotting tooth, which the tongue
nags at uncontrollably;
at last like a dull ache, fading

— Bryher seen in terms of pain.

23

As a child she rode camels,
deciphered hieroglyphics on tombs,
learned the language of bazaars

— all this wearing
heavy flannel petticoats
and proper white gloves. Later,
imprisoned in a school, a
family, she turned
against herself that
Egyptian energy. Fiercely
her will controlled whatever it could
and buried the rest.

She bargained me her heart
with a trader's honesty
wrapped in a language I could not understand.

24

But what was the bargain? Bryher
needed me to tell a lie, provide
a mask of respectability, a pass
from her parents' prison. But me —

I was already booked on a boat
working my way to China.
I could have come to Paris like a rumour
years later, out of the East....

What was the bargain? What was the price?
Bryher twisting in my hands
like an eel escaping
the charge of her own electricity.

25

I will not say I did not love her;
I will not say I did: the truth
is long forgotten by us both.

In any case it played little part
in our manoeuvres. If I had known
how rich exactly she was — but she could not
afford me that knowledge. At the same time
she had to offer me at least a passage
as far as France, speaking strictly
in terms of business, while I
guessed at levels of meaning suppressed
and cryptic as crossword clues.

And so on. Once you believe
the lies you tell yourself to confirm
the lies you're told by another,
there's no way out of the maze.

On St. Valentine's Day we were married.
A paper down in Los Angeles hired
two hack actors, dressed them up,
and took a photograph they claimed
gave a true picture of our love-match.
It did.

26

Bill Williams gaped like a stricken fish;
H.D. remained inscrutable. We toasted fortune
and sailed for Europe, twelve days married,

my bride still virgin.

II EUROPE (1921-1940)

And what iz gone wrong with McAlmon? The kid just playing the fool, or wotever? Too bad some of his best have been printed, though hardly more than privately printed. I hope he ain't gone plumb to hell.

Ezra Pound, 1935

So I went into exile

rootless / deracinate

and Europe
shoved a glass into my hand
shifting over at the bar
to make room for one more
drunken Ulysses
heading for his ten years' war.

Sir John at the head of the table
never raised his voice, and never
exceeded two glasses of brandy.
He had no need of either. Bryher
shrank back to the shadows where I
first saw her, rendered nothing
inside the darkness of this house.

On the walls were paintings of geese,
woodlands and cattle: the choice was Sir John's,
feeling no need to follow fashion,
but settled in the comfort of mute beasts.
His son in later years
became a recluse and studied rodents.

Her Ladyship's pale arms like patches
of furtive moonlight lay in the gloom.
They had lived together for years
before being married: now the richest
taxpayer in England feared her still,
her deafness, her obstinate fits, her fierce
hold on her children – only matched
by his obsessive jealousy. Nothing
changed in that house from day to year.

On the first night Her Ladyship came
gliding into our room without asking
to see her darlings together in bed –
our bodies rigid with pretence, maintaining
an inch against the possibility
of touch – while Her Ladyship beamed
and left us to the darkness of the house.

Sir John at the head of the table,
the mute beasts watching from the walls,
and Bryher dissolving down
to a single strand
of will.

London was fog and paranoia:
restrictions at every turn, you shouldn't
speak in front of the servants, you can't
enter without a tie, a bowler
is the only permissible hat for Hyde Park ...

I dined with Wyndham Lewis at
the Eiffel Tower (in London miming
Parisian grace), and he denounced
all the rumours I'd never heard
against him; then caught my sleeve
before I could speak, and gesturing
to the empty table behind him
whispered 'Shh — they're listening.'

Then Eliot the governess
wrote me a letter in his careful prose
warning me to avoid in Paris
a certain 'congeries' of people,
time-wasting and futile — only
Prufrock could have used that word,
precise and dry as skin too long
stretched under lamplight.

31

Paris was queen of those dying cities
– London, Rome, Berlin –
Paris around the slate-grey Seine,
city of silent memory, magnet
of possibilities.

I never could leave
or stay in that city, pulled
by poles of rejection one
half of each year
away to wherever the moment's boredom
suggested diversion, but always returning

October along the river, gold
of trees in the Luxembourg gardens,
the grey light seizing clear
a hold on my erring mind
turning it like a magnet's eye
to the one fixed point, true north,
Paris under a wintry dawn,
its buildings etched like acid on the sky.

32

Rue Delambre
Rue du Montparnasse
Rue Campagne Première

Rue Notre Dame des Champs
Rue du Cardinal Lemoine
Rue de Fleurus

Rue de Vaugirard
Rue du Cherche Midi
Rue Rousselet

Rue Broca
Rue de la Gaîté
Passage d'Enfer

Rue de l'Arrivée
Rue du Départ

In Paris I wrote about Dakota:
nothing strange in that. The years of dust
and the burning sky
were still as close as pen and paper.
The foreign language entered my ears
as echoes of American.

Revise, revise, they told me:
polish your style, make shining phrases
glittering, concise as telegrams.
Like Hemingway, who always tried
to make you believe he had fine perceptions
by cutting them out of his prose.
Or governess Eliot, deus in absentia,
refining anguish to a whimpered quotation.

But I was writing of the mid-West plains
where the sky is endless, horizon
perpetual doorstep to possibility.
I needed no lies or evasions, I wanted only
contact
with the whole multifarious world.

Stein told me once my work
had this at least: abundance.
I think she meant it as an insult:
I understand it, still, as praise.

34

Glow, glaux, glaucoma,
grey-eyed Athena, goddess of wisdom,
blind
       — the pain increasing, he
would turn to me: 'Bob, for
pity's sake, get me home!' —
                     Astarte,
Esther, estarr, dark star. Ineluctable.

The left eye sinister, bound in black
stuffed full of cocaine: but then
lilt of an old-time song, white wine,
his fine Irish tenor, the voice betrayed
by moments of pain, his patron goddess.

'A hasty bunch, McAlmon.'
The office boy's revenge.

Long evenings of his gentle humour,
no one like Joyce for a joke or a song;
shall we try — what say you? — to sample
every drink on this menu?

And Nora: 'I guess the man's a genius,
but hasn't he a dirty mind?'

Black wine, glaucoma. Pressure on the nerve:
the pain of sight
in a world, in a word, in a work
in progress.

And do you think I didn't take
my own title
          with a pinch of salt?
Being geniuses together
is no easy matter: I don't possess
a patent alarm-bell system
like Alice B. Toklas, I'm not
convinced about anyone, least
of all myself. But I won't allow
anyone else to tell me either
who was or who wasn't, Stein
or Joyce or Jolas, Hemingway or me.

Sit us all at one table
with a bottle of wine
and see who lasts the longest then.
Montparnasse in the first light of dawn
has a kind of hard-edged honesty
it makes all judgements lies.

36

'Knock on wood,' said Bricktop,
'Crutcher's shot dead.' Early morning
after a hard night's drinking. Less
than two hours earlier, up there
at Bricktop's nightclub in Montmartre,
Leon Crutcher playing piano
sweet and pure and clean, a melody
like the line of Brancusi's statues.
The dawn edging grey and nostalgic
into the morning of Quatorze Juillet.

Crutcher was a black man, could've been
a concert pianist otherwise;
he was killed by a jealous mistress, white,
no jury in France would convict.

He must have stood before her, caught
on the thread of his music still, remembering
every note in exact relation: watched
the bullet starting from her gun
its curious voyage into his head.
'Go on. I dare you. Shoot if you dare.'
His own voice playing descant to his fear.

'Knock on wood,' said Bricktop.
The morning's dead. Why is it
always so, the death of musicians
is more than just the ending
of their song?

Quote:
From an h'English printer
to an English publisher.

We beg to acknowledge receipt
of your letter dated
August 2nd and the copy
for book. We are returning
the same to you as you
have quite evidently mistaken
the standing that our firm
enjoys in the Printing World.
We have been established over
60 years and do not remember
ever being asked to place
such literature before
our workspeople before,
and you can rest assured
that we are not
going to begin now. Thanking
you for your kind enquiry. Yours
faithfully, unquote. A legal
handwriting, blotted in sand,
a dead
         signature.

The first book
printed
held in my hands —

Darantière of Dijon,
Contact Editions.

Looking at it now, I find
a hundred mistakes, the printers' French
unequal battle with my American
speech: *A Hasty Bunch*

of stories which pretended nothing
except to be
                    what they were
the record of life

not writing but contact
direct as a camera's
circular eye.

39

In dead Berlin the daughters
and sons of the nobility
in pure politeness offered themselves
for a million marks or a couple of dollars
to whatever whim you demanded
their bodies to submit to.

Nothing was left but a sense
of minimal honour: a name
held in their eyes, a space preserved
from which they could watch, dispassionate,
their young clean bodies like machines

performing in darkened rooms, or pressed
against the sweating stone of alleyways
far in the dark from boulevards
down which their Prussian fathers rode

unter den Linden, Ehre.

40

The bitter mechanics of love
for a man or woman, I've known both,
are never more than a night's pretence,
gestures of tenderness betrayed
by the twist of the mind standing back
in mocking despair. It is not good
but only unavoidable, to follow each desire
straight through to its futility,
waking in the morning white as cocaine
sick in Berlin in a rented room.
My back is turned to last night's lover,
whose sex I cannot quite determine,
there is little to feel but a turgid anger
at nothing I can name. It is easy enough
and only human not to condemn;
the wounded pass before my eyes
in travesties of honour: let me take
nothing of love away from them
as long as I can bear the shame
of my own presence here, the sham
hollow rotten pretence
of being more than a proud cold eye
trained like a rifle on the captive world.

41

I marched on Rome with Mussolini, arriving
the same day though by different routes.
His thugs were swarming in the streets,
force-feeding castor oil to those who failed
to sing the right words to a Fascist song
or raise their hands in the new salute.
Once watching a parade go by, I had
my hat knocked off my disrespectful head.

I've often wondered where they come from,
the wave of sadists, cretins, pimps,
who greet each new dictatorship, and crush
delightedly beneath their heels their own
identical twins of the previous reign.
History teaches them nothing — nor us, it seems,
applauding power when a gangster's hand
waves in the sky the imperial gesture,
his orator's voice ringing hollow as bells.

For a while as a tourist I followed
the guidebook round of ruined monuments
till polite pretence turned into farce:
too many ruins for the eye to hold,
Il Duce in the Colosseum watching
the games of death that raged
in the arena of my own sick heart.

42

Broad alley of golden
trees: the Pantheon dome
framed in their branches, grey
as air condensed into
sculptor's stone. The perfect
circle of pond, where
toy boats sail, surrounded
by rings of balustrades
and avenues. Luxembourg
Gardens, a formal
completion, the broad
alley of golden trees
west to the gates, to the exit
onto the Rue de Fleurus.

43

Stein is German for stone: immutable,
moving as slowly as glaciers,
churning the earth to repeated rubble
under their pitiless advance.

What is there to say about Gertrude?
For forty years she was one
idea of Paris: upon her walls
the visible world made manifest
surrounded the slow relentless
trudge of her conversation. Alice
was lodged like a shard of flint
embedded in this progression.

The voice that counted the years
of a century passing, turned
like an echo-chamber in on itself,
heard only reverberations, beat
of the mind like a drumskin stretched
over a hollow thought.

I liked her at first, exchanging
recommendations for Trollope, accounts
of travels into distant places we
had both intuited. But she
had seldom any need for friendship,
only for adulation — well,
I'm scarcely the disciple kind.

continued ...

She was there when I came, when
I left she was there: Gertrude
and Alice unmoving, serene
'like a monument seated on patience,'
the words flowing on like
lava congealing, gradual
and imperturbable: a slow
reduction of consciousness into
her terms of time, the continuous
present, tense, and repeating

word.

45

Then the good doctor came
to Paris from Paterson,
prescription pad filled
with famous names.
Show me some writers, Bob,
take me to Gertrude Stein's

and they insulted each other
firmly, with great politeness —
'But writing, Doctor, is not your métier' —
the clink of teacups rattling
a shade too loudly in the outraged room.

And now some French ones, Bob,
Dadaists, Surrealists, don't you know
anyone here? Fakes, I told him,
phonies, forget them, come on
let's visit James Joyce for a bottle of wine
and a whimsical Irish song.

In 1924, for God's sake,
you didn't come to Paris
to waste your time on the French!

46

And when we met it was cautiously
reaching for friendship back
to the river's pride.
For years in the turning seasons
he was the true direction
I never could flow alongside.

He saw in my eyes a mirror
reflecting the dawn, but nothing
was living behind them. He asked
questions about my marriage
as a friend but also a doctor
diagnosing some disease.

At last he returned to his country,
Paterson beneath the falls,
to hours in his surgery writing
prescription blank poems. I left
three days before his final party,
left Paris and headed south
for somewhere I could write alone.
I've never thought the word Goodbye
is worth the breath of saying.

47

The word for peace in 29 languages
flowed like a river's murmur through
the melodious voice of Mr. Joyce
reciting for the reverential few.

Rats. Linguistics doesn't impress me
although I bowed my head, and clasped
my hands in an attitude of prayer.
A Frenchman slapped me in the face
claiming later he thought my gesture
ridiculed his wife's thick ankles.

I'm talking of the tolerance
of audiences. Eliot came
over from London to hear Pound's opera,
sat at the back and slipped away
untouched by contact with his friends.
Ezra himself hung upside down
from the upper balcony screaming praise
against the din of abuse at Antheil's
player pianos and airplane propellors.

The only thing that stopped them dead
at any party, any bar, was always
McAlmon's Chinese Opera, a long
high wordless toneless wail
that filled the empty sky inside my head
and got me thrown out on the street
to seek the perfect audience of dawn.

48

I suffered regular
visits to London, where Bryher
was working over H.D.'s child
(they called The Lump)
reproducing her own neuroses
with loving care.
                    And meanwhile
Mamma Darling relapsed into rage
refusing to go for a drive in the car,
and Sir John to his daughter's rare delight
told of a long-delayed revenge, of waiting
fifteen years to drive from England
someone who had crossed him, and who now
could be allowed to come back home.
All this was most instructive
for a lad like me from
South Dakota.

When finally the divorce was decided
Sir John wrote a cheque, Her Ladyship wept,
and Bryher coldly shook my hand
as if we had just been introduced
by some well-meaning friend.

49

At night the river
runs black as thought
beneath the Pont du Carrousel

a crazy-go-round of
faces reflected, my
sister's tears

this city where the wind has never
dried her eyes.

Surrealists in prose were dull, in poetry worse,
but they could be fun in theatres, attacking
authors, actors, and most of all
each other. I used to watch them in action —
Breton the commander-in-chief, the wild duck
Aragon — from the bar at the back of the hall
in the old Cigale: vantage-point of the true
discriminating critics. The audience yelled
abuse at the stage, and the drinkers replied
by abusing the audience. Meanwhile oblivious

the actors like saints pursued their ritual
self-enclosed in space and time. Cocteau
directed *Romeo and Juliet* in black:
the actors in black against black curtains
visible only by stark white limbs
drawn in Sumerian style, embroidered
over the blackness they wore. Like X-rays
the ghosts of these long-dead adolescents
moved in the void of poetry

while I at the bar downed a dozen whiskies
and yelled for silence till my ear-drums broke.

51

And then that evening the workers came
from the city we never knew:
the slaughterhouses of Pantin, the long
grey stretches of the river east:
out of the Faubourg St. Antoine
and narrow stinking alleys of Plaisance:

to Montparnasse like a foreign land,
the 'playground of the idle rich'
les américains, les assassins:

moving in squads down the Boulevard
smashing tables on the Dôme terrasse
manhandling customers in La Rotonde
mixing wine and blood on the floors
till it spilled to the street like justice done
tonight by any means against
les assassins, les américains:

like hammers struck on rusted iron,
like axes biting rotten wood,
out of the city we never knew
the night that Sacco and Vanzetti died.

52

Come closer. The desert wind
blows straight from the sun. I've seen it rise
all colours here: mad Harry's god
as lurid as a gunshot wound
destroying the temple.

He said he could mix me a drink
to bring on delirium: I stayed cold sober
and watched him swallow fire.
He was always a ghost, a deserter
from anything I called reality.

The sun out here that burns my eyes
and shrivels skin to skeleton
must be his revenge for my scorn.
I despised him then, and resented his death
as an unfair trick, the comic Fool
become suddenly Lear, on a wheel of fire,
spinning to chaos.

They tell me that two hours went by
between the girl's death and his own.
In all the time I've died out here
I've thought of Harry Crosby often:
I know now why he chose the sun;
I know now why he waited in his turn.

53

Pascin hanging in his room
his body revolving shadows
over his paintings:

the artists of suicide
will tell you
the trick is only
to choose your time
and satisfy your audience,
leave them
asking for more.

But other deaths are hidden,
there is no audience. If
there are no good reasons for living,
then I believe there are none
for dying either.

There was the Japanese painter,
Toda,
who always seemed to be starving
to death, which indeed he was
and finally did,
alone in his room, too proud
to ask a franc
from any of his friends who squandered
fortunes in Montparnasse.

For those with no good reasons
Paris was the hiding-place:
a public life, a secret death.

Kay Boyle: first time I saw her
thin and scared, her garish makeup
ineptly smudged across her face;
all eyes and bones (her awkward nose
broken in childhood), fierce intensity
of silence at a café table, shy
but with words waiting for their chance to grow.

She loved the dead
and dying: Ernest Walsh,
high in the splendid gaiety of those
who know their death from close at hand,
he claimed her with their daughter's birth
then bled his lungs out in the mountain air.

And she sensed something dead in me
to which she turned like a wave to shore
crashing on rocks: dead long ago,
stillborn perhaps in South Dakota,
drowned in the Hudson River, drunk away
in any of a thousand all-night bars,
indifferently smothered in Berlin,
lost in a poem I could never write,
or hooded blank in Bryher's eyes.

One evening out at Crosby's mill
she started quoting my old poetry
as if she could create me whole.
Nothing, I told her, there is nothing here,
nothing to love or be loved by:
a void, a failure, an apology.
She stood and watched me in the moon:
pale, pearl and seashell, on her face
the skin stretched tight as bone.

There is a death I owe which she may claim
whenever she forgives the time.

Now for a spot of melodrama:
a dinner party for Ezra Pound,
the guest of honour to my left
dried out by the Italian sun,
the spur of his stubborn beard
jutting fiercely into the argument
on usury and 'eccy-nomics' —

and at the table next to us
a young Maltese I slightly knew,
crazed on cocaine and Lautréamont,
was yelling at a lily English boy
I took to be his lover by the tender way
he flung him through the window. Then

he rose to his feet with a long
stiletto blade poised in his hand
and made for Ezra. We were both
boxed in by chairs, tight at the table,
unable to stand or turn. I grabbed
for his wrist, and the circling knife
sliced my coat-sleeve, grazing my arm,
just missing the vein.

Then someone hit him with a wine carafe,
he slumped to my feet, I took the knife
before the police arrived and hid it —
no point that I could see in sending him
to get beaten by guards in a Paris jail.

Meanwhile the author of *The Cantos*
had bowed his face to meet the table
as if it were a headsman's block:
and on the crown of his fierce red hair
like a matador's hat was resting
my severed sleeve.

Where are they now, the legendary
drinkers of years gone by?
Nina Hamnett, Flossie Martin,
Djuna Barnes, Mina Loy ...
Where are the nights that met the dawn
cold-eyed and sober as we strolled
the early morning markets at Les Halles,
or breakfasted with sleepy whores?
Where are the songs that Nina sang
in her British accent, genteelly obscene,
at 4 a.m. in the Falstaff bar?
Echoes fading from the dark oak walls ...

The hell with it. Time passes,
that's all that happens;
the body rots a little, and the mind
fills up with sand. One last
romantic chorus for you all:

où sont les neiges d'antan, old friends,
where are the years downtown?

57

The decade was dead, and everyone
knew it except for the two
susceptible boys. For Glassco and Taylor
everything was new again: the first
night at the Falstaff, the actual thrill
of meeting James Joyce, or even
parading off to Gertrude Stein's.
They were as fresh as flowers of April
blooming in early September.

For Buffy, to be cynical was one
of the social graces: I envied the ease
of disillusion worn like a coat
with impeccable taste. Yet he was open,
naive as a child, susceptible,
spending his body like a man
might spend his money who felt ill at ease
at being rich when all his friends were poor.

Was I ever as young as he was? Could
I ever have acted like him, that night
out of jealous boredom I attacked Kay Boyle
ripping her silly illusions to threads
for all the bar to hear, and she threw
a beer glass at me, which missed
but drenched young Glassco, and he dropped
his head to the counter and cried?

Then on the beach at Nice he posed
his perfect body on the hard round stones

and in the photograph surviving
his eyes look down
as if the stones could puzzle out
a self-sufficiency of being
graceful as epigrams, and firm
as careless muscles on his youthful arm

and meanwhile I am gazing far
out of the frame with an angry glare
as always, at nothing at all.

59

To hell with Paris,
with it's buildings that don't give a damn
for the people who happen to be there
this particular century,
its buildings impassive as stone
its streets that gather the years
its river that runs through your mind like time —

to hell with Paris,
the city of light be damned,
implacable, relentless, forgiving
nothing from all your wasted days,
I've had enough

of its inescapable
inhuman   unbearable
eternal

beauty

A decade of discontent,
of restless travelling — Paris
no longer the centre — back and forth
across the ocean and the continent —
just as I used to search the Paris bars
nightlong for someone who was missing,
anyone, to make the evening whole —

ten years' futility. Beginning
1930 in Mexico, drifting north to
Hollywood, New York, by year's end
back to Paris, not staying there,
a Riviera summer, then to madness
Munich, Berlin, the Nazis in the streets;
summer of '32 Majorca, then
a year in Spain, near Barcelona, everywhere
signs of decay, the rot setting in;
back in Paris in time for Stavisky
6th February 1934, eleven dead
in the place of concord; after that
writing in Strasbourg, crossing to London,
publishers all the same refusal,
late in the year returned to New York.
Decade's midpoint, sunk in Depression.
1935 in Texas, El Paso,
then California, '36 a haze
of border crossings, back and forth
to San Francisco, Mexico, L.A.,
a dreary catalogue; April of '37
wasted in Santa Barbara, nothing there,
crossed back again in June
through Paris east to Switzerland,
August in Austria, through the Balkans,
then nowhere else to go except back
to Paris; London in '38, my book
published, attacked, ignored;

continued ...

return to France, continuous wandering
round the west country, Rochefort,
Chatelaillon, Maintenon, establishing
a house of sorts in Dampierre, which was
efficiently looted in '39, October,
twenty years of books and papers
disappeared. Futility. The Nazis
marching in Paris, the decade closed
in war and murder. Fall of 1940
American passport to Lisbon, the
stink of neutrality, easy way home.

62

Meanwhile Bryher in Switzerland
lived in a cloak and dagger world
she must have enjoyed, of intrigue
deception and danger. Her home
was clearing-house for hunted refugees
escaping Germany by secret routes:
each new arrival at her door
a man marked for the death-camps, or
perhaps a spy. When war broke out
she fled to France, and then was forced
south to Lisbon, just like me.

(Suppose that I had met her there —
two strangers in a line of refugees —
sitting on her suitcase waiting
for some uncertain ship to take her home.
Her eyes are hollowed by dark rings
like targets in her narrow face;
her weary voice searches for something
polite to say to this memory.
'And what have you been up to, Robert?
How have you spent these last ten years?')

Her country was not neutral, she
had nowhere else to go
but back to London, to her father's house
already shaken by the falling bombs.

Lisbon seen from the sea
like a jewelled door
closing on Europe —

the Castle riding its spur of rock
above the city, pure white birds
flamingoes and peacocks, haunting its walls;
the colonnades of the Black Horse Square
meeting the waterfront with high
Venetian dignity; and farther west,
whining white as the Castle's birds,
the Belém tower, point of departure
for all explorers, point of return.

I preferred the narrow streets
that twist beneath the Castle's height,
the dark Alfama, the unchanging town
outlasting earthquakes, where the women sing
fado, the music of travellers,
for those who may never return

setting out westward past the Belém tower
where Tagus opens to the setting sea.

64

III DESERT HOT SPRINGS (1940-1956)

'Life begins, they say, at forty.... It ought to be interesting when it really gets underway.'

Robert McAlmon, 1934

I have so dreamed you all:

captains of possibility
outriders of despair

67

I missed both wars — not
that I'm much of a soldier — in fact,
for all the misery I'm glad
still to be sticking around —
but I feel like I sidestepped history,
the century came like a circus to town
and I got cheated on the sideshows.

1918 my volunteer days
pissed away in a training camp,
a desert not unlike this one;
1940 I ran into exile
kicked out of Europe's back door.

There was the lie I told to Glassco,
that I'd joined the Canadian Army
and then deserted — something
there was from which I deserted, I can't
deny. 'The Canadian Army'
sounds as good a disguise as any
for something I'd rather not name.

68

No phoenix rises
from the desert here: I'm reduced
to that kind of pun.
My brothers gave me a job —
no one is after all less trained
for making a living than someone
whose business has been no more than living,
an unpublished writer —
for Southwest Surgical Supply
in Phoenix Arizona, selling trusses,
and for ten years
that's how I lived.

You know how trusses work?
They hold things in —
useless, decaying things —
they hold things in
until they die.

69

The body's dis-ease:
tumours, ulcers, hernias,
cancers pale as the sky at dawn,
decay of growth
turned inward and turned foul.

Ten years of dealing with deformity:
polite discretion, the salesman's smile
that will not dare
to laugh, or retch, or fantasize
unsterilised knives

slicing these rancid mockeries of flesh.

70

When I had money, McAlimony,
it was easy to give, and now is no need
to list the years and names.
If I can take pride, it is only
in gifts I could give from the poor
underwear-salesman's pittance of paycheque,
the truss-seller's salary. So

I will mention this one: at Christmas
1942 I sent ten dollars,
all I could manage, to Djuna Barnes
author of *Nightwood,* who
needed it. As for myself

throughout that season I sat alone
enclosed in a Phoenix room, and in
a vacuum of sound
waiting for the telephone to ring
and some dead poet to call me
out of the shrivelled air.

71

Once, for three weeks
I gave up speaking —
not a word passed my lips
or my sand-rubbed eyes.
I did not read, or listen to the radio;
I trained my eyes to avoid
the words on packages and signs.
I gave up thinking.

I lived for three weeks a pure
non-verbal existence: things
proclaimed themselves as truly objects,
irreducible to sound. I moved
among them like a silent animal,
I did not call myself a name
or invade their own mute privacy.
The books on my shelves
were exotic plants, with pure white leaves
and small black flowers.

I had no special reason
for starting words again: I picked them up
like clothes discarded on the floor
by the side of the bed three weeks before —
unwashed, as soiled as ever,
the sweat dried in their careless folds.

72

On a Phoenix radio, gritty with sand,
voices fell like ghosts from the air:
the Liberation of Paris, the news
reporter's voice is cracked with emotion,
for he has legends to tell.

On the embassy roof in a hail of bullets
the toga-clad figure of Raymond Duncan
waving the stars and stripes.
Hemingway as usual the hero
knocking on Sylvia Beach's door
then setting off to liberate
the cellar of the Ritz.
And somewhere in the south of France
Gertrude and Alice indestructible
surface to a surfeit of G.I.s.

The hand that reaches out
to turn the radio off
is parchment skin and hollow bone.
The mind has already shut itself off,
but somewhere in the darkness between stations
a voice is screaming down
the airwaves of the long dead years

McAlmon's Chinese Opera.

73

Ezra in St. Elizabeth's:
I had to laugh when they called him mad —
for who is sane, Hiroshima?
children of Nagasaki, who will judge?
Crystal sands where the desert flowers,
where is the pride of words
when such a deed is 'civilised'?

Each morning I smell the wind
like a dog, suspiciously,
remembering the ugly sign
we scratched upon the retina of sky.

At Los Alamos they tell me
after the bomb the desert bloomed
strange flowers on the sand,
metamorphosis, black stars.

It is as if the eye
were to splinter into itself
so that all we could see were scars
and patches of light

like holding to your eye a child's
kaleidoscope on fire.

75

The heat reduces
everything to rock, and rock
to sand. The acid air
bites corrosive into bone;
the eye is narrowed down
to a small burnt hole.

Come in
under the shadow of this red rock,
how Eliot would have loved
this sterile landscape:
no shadow left, and soon enough
no rock.

(I remember Dakota winters
 blue skies as hard as diamond,
 sunlight mirrored on the snow.
 I want to be preserved in ice
 with my dead eyes wide open,
 frozen blue.)

76

William Carlos
Williams told me
I should have been Billy
the Kid.

Hot desert night
Desert Hot Springs / Fort Sumner
no guns in my hands.
Come on in,
Dr. Pat Garrett.

77

On the bridge across to Mexico
a lump of huddled blanket
aroused his curiosity. It was
an occasion for speech. The doctor

naive as always, exclaimed
'Wow!' at a passing perfume
when all it was, was whores.

Tequila five cents a glass, across
the bridge back to El Paso:
spit both ways in the running stream.
He wrote to me from the train

saying things might change.
He got 'The Desert Music' out of it
and all I got, was whores.

78

He sent it first to Mexico,
Cuernavaca, where I'd been
a month before. From there,
like a bomb in a brown paper parcel,
it followed my addresses round
until October, Desert Hot Springs, when
I came here it was waiting.
The doctor's autobiography

took the old scars, the Bryher scars,
and with a scalpel's delicacy
cut them open, left them to bleed
and fester in his casual eye.
Thirty years of what we stood for
in one uncalculated blunder
shattered like crystal glass
in the pitch of a toneless scream.

For Bryher, pain was domestic convention;
she lived by its rules, and could win
any game it demanded. I thought
I had learned her techniques —
I wore my friendships light as laughter,
nothing struck home. I was wrong.

His eye turned in on God knows what
mirror of pride or self-disgust,
he saw things crooked, and saw me
cold as a case-book diagnosis
deprived of my last defence
against the years it would take me
to die outside his company.

He sent it first to Mexico
and it followed me like the light
from a burnt-out star
that is dead already a million years
only we don't know that
yet.

Europe, these years,
considered as mythology —
a time more true than time —
while I pursued my distinguished
medical career. Ending at last
— too sick to sell to the sick —
at the corner of 2nd and Cactus
here on the desert's rim.

It was pointless to think of returning — Paris
had become no more than a map,
streetnames and picture postcards, no-one
remembers me now. I could walk
all night through Montparnasse without seeing
my name in the sudden mirror
of any familiar face.

Paris is now the city
where truly I am dying: here
the sun holds time in suspension,
my body in the dry air does not rot;
but in Paris my death hurries on
and my eyes are pressed shut
by mists that hang over the Seine
like dancers every dawn.

What Pound was after: nothing less
than everything, spread
throughout a poem that could never end,
being more than even he
and his crazy life could comprehend.

This was the true abundance
the century aimed for: not the concise
particular image, shining
caged within limits — but Contact
wide as the eagle's eye, uniting
continents and centuries.

I sit in this room with my books
(as many as I have saved)
gathering sand from the wind all night
clouding the dawn —

and Ezra in his madhouse rages
caged on the edge of the sea,
wearing his life, my severed sleeve,
like a clown's cap now
on his head that will never bow
(unlike my own)
beneath the witness of decaying years.

81

The ratio of everything
I wanted to what I achieved
I am not calculating
enough to compute. When death
is considered, not as a fiction
but as something closer
than dawn or tomorrow, you know
there is nothing to give
back to the generous daily
provision of breath: no words,
no construction of words,
that will comfort the fine isolation
of speaking your name
into the desert of emptying
echoing dark. What I see
is my sister's shadow
fallen over the page where my hand
faltered in writing
the poem the dawn demanded
clear
as the neon skeleton of fire.

82

Begin laughing
when you read the lines
of my death in print.
Say that I knew
before the finale
the twist of the lips and the bitter grin
of a man who drinks sand
and rinses his eyes
in answers and acid.
When you know that the desert
has eaten my skin
and you hear all the posthumous
lies, begin laughing
to scour out my name
from your memory's substitute
stone.

83

I am watching my face
in the mirror collapsing:
not even my eyes
can keep their distance.

This is my hand, I remember
contact and touch — yes even
Bryher's thin body
taut as electric wire — my hand,
if I cut off my hand

would the wrist inherit
its devious memories, deaths
of the bodies Berlin provided
cheap, without honour or shame?

The dance of deceptions
plays over my face, and my eyes
are like letters on fire
curling to ashes.
The mirror looks the other way.

Why should it be Bryher now
my body remembers
seeing her naked as lightning,
white as a summer storm?

84

Now it is years
since I slept with a woman
or with a man.
Now it is years
since I even bothered to please
myself with my hand.

My body is shrunken and useless
dry as Coyote's turd
in the desert sand.

85

Shuffle of dust,
an old man's slippers moving
across the room, from wall to wall,
like a prisoner pacing his cell.
You can sit where you like:
the chairs are all the same.

Shuffle of dust,
the years fall through my hands
like playing-cards. The names
are second-hand books on sale
for a dime or a nickel.
You have heard me out.

What I never wanted
was pity — I will not accept
the luxury of failure.
Montparnasse in the first light of dawn
has still that hard-edged honesty
it makes all judgements lies.

86

The year is 1956
I am 60 years old
Almost everyone I can think of
is dead
And I am dying of pneumonia

My name is Robert McAlmon
I published eleven books
verse and fiction and autobiography
I wrote many more
which are lost

I live in a room
at the corner of 2nd and Cactus
in a town called Desert Hot Springs
My sister visits me
My mother died in 1943

I am the famous writer
I am the famous traveller
I am the famous seller of trusses
I am the famous footnote
on other people's lives

My sister visits me
I am 60 years old
It is Friday the 2nd of February
1956

Oh loving darkness leave me not alone

Robert McAlmon was born in Kansas on March 9th, 1896. His father was
an Irishman who had emigrated to Canada; his mother, Bess Urquhart,
was born in Chatham, Ontario. His father was a Presbyterian minister
who travelled around the American Mid-West; McAlmon spent most of
his youth in South Dakota, until in 1910 the family moved to Minneapolis. In 1918, McAlmon enlisted in the Air Corps, but never got
farther than training camp in San Diego. (He later encouraged an apoc-
ryphal story that he had joined — and then deserted — the Canadian
Army.) After the death of his father in 1917, his mother moved to Los
Angeles. After the war, McAlmon briefly attended the University of
Southern California; but in 1920 he left, and headed for Chicago.

In Chicago, he began his literary contacts, meeting the poet Emanuel
Carnevali, whom he was to support, years later, when Carnevali was
dying of encephalitis in Italy. Later in 1920, McAlmon moved to New
York, where he became friendly with the painter Marsden Hartley, and
with a young doctor called William Carlos Williams — this latter a friendship that was to be one of the foundations of McAlmon's life for the next
thirty years. Together with Williams, he founded the little magazine
Contact, which first appeared in December, 1920. During this period,
McAlmon was living on a garbage scow on the Hudson River, and sup-
porting himself by posing nude for art students at Cooper Union.

In September, 1920, Williams took his friend to meet the poet H.D.,
who was travelling in company with a young English woman who called
herself Bryher. Her real name was Winifred Ellerman, and her father, Sir
John Ellerman, was a shipping magnate and one of the wealthiest men in
England. The facts surrounding McAlmon's marriage to Bryher are
obscure, and the subject of much speculation. Both he and Bryher are
exceptionally reticent about it in their memoirs — a fact which in itself
suggests that the relationship held more emotional conflict than either
of them was willing to face, or admit. The 'official' version is that it was a
marriage of convenience. Bryher was a lively and independent young
woman, being slowly strangled by the conformist pressures of her family
position; for her, a husband was little more than a nominal passport,
allowing her to live and travel independently of her parents. For McAlmon, marriage to Bryher offered a passage to Europe, and ultimately a
great deal of money — but he always insisted, most people believe truth-
fully, that he did not know before he married her how wealthy Bryher's
family was.

Whatever the motives behind the marriage, it was, emotionally, a disaster. The most extreme view is that of McAlmon's sister Victoria, who later said that 'the word "love" was synonymous to "lie" for him because one woman made it seem that way.' Thirty years later, William Carlos Williams' tactless handling of the affair in his *Autobiography* was enough to destroy McAlmon's deepest friendship. McAlmon, who was probably bisexual, never in his life developed a lasting or rewarding sexual relationship with any other person.

McAlmon and Bryher were married in New York on February 14th (St. Valentine's Day!), 1921, and twelve days later they sailed for Europe. After a brief stay in London with his bride's highly neurotic family, McAlmon naturally gravitated to Paris. Although he was to travel almost constantly for the next two decades, Paris was his centre, as it was for so many Americans of his generation.

In Paris, McAlmon quickly established himself on the literary scene. He became especially close to James Joyce, who enjoyed his drinking companionship as much as his short stories – stories whose unpolished, rough and ready directness appealed to Joyce. He suggested to McAlmon the title for his first collection, *A Hasty Bunch*. After the manuscript was indignantly turned down by an English printer, McAlmon had it printed himself, by Darantière of Dijon (the printer of *Ulysses*), as the first of the Contact Editions. McAlmon used Sylvia Beach's bookshop, Shakespeare and Company, as the address for the press.

After a rocky start, McAlmon established a long-standing friendship with Ezra Pound, who always championed McAlmon's writing. It was at Pound's home in Rapallo that he met Ernest Hemingway, whom he initially liked. They went on a trip to Spain (at McAlmon's expense), and Contact Editions published Hemingway's first book, *Three Stories and Ten Poems* (1923); but later the friendship dissolved into rivalry and bitter enmity. An initial friendship with Gertrude Stein also came to grief during a complex dispute over the publication of the first (and for forty years the only) complete edition of *The Making of Americans* – which remains, nevertheless, the Contact Press's most impressive achievement.

McAlmon's travels took him to Berlin, which in 1921 was the centre of European post-war depravity; but out of the hopeless lives of the drug addicts and homosexuals of Berlin's nightclubs, McAlmon fashioned his most powerful prose fiction, the brilliant stories which make up *Distinguished Air: Grim Fairy Tales,* published by Bill Bird's Three Mountains Press in Paris in 1925.

McAlmon's contacts in Paris were mainly with American and English writers; his knowledge of the French literary scene was severely limited, as William Carlos Williams discovered, to his disappointment, during a visit in 1924. McAlmon had a low opinion of Surrealism — in fact, as the years went on, he seemed to have a low opinion of most successful literary trends and figures. His own reputation was fast being eclipsed by the success of other writers, like Hemingway, whom he considered (with, it may be argued, some justification) to be his inferiors. The bitterness which was to characterise so much of his later life was setting in.

In 1926, the public friction of his marriage to Bryher ended in divorce. Sir John gave him a handsome settlement, which promptly earned him in Montparnasse the nickname of 'McAlimony.' In fact, McAlmon was widely if quietly generous with the Ellerman money, using it not only for the Contact Press but also to subsidise many of his friends and fellow writers, including Joyce and Carnevali.

As the decade drew to its close, it became apparent that McAlmon was not going to get the recognition he deserved. His work was admired by Pound, Williams, and Katherine Anne Porter, and was especially praised by Ernest Walsh, the young and dying editor of *This Quarter*; another fervent and life-long supporter was Kay Boyle. But his relations with the major avant-garde periodical, Eugene Jolas' *transition,* were always cool, and the American publishing houses remained closed to him — partly because of vicious opposition from Scott Fitzgerald, but also partly because McAlmon blew his own opportunity during a lunch with Scribner's editor, Maxwell Perkins, to whom he did nothing but repeat slanderous gossip against Ernest Hemingway.

McAlmon renewed his somewhat tenuous connections to Canada with friendships, at the end of the decade, with Morley Callaghan, and with John Glassco and Graeme Taylor. One of the most vivid and brilliant sketches of McAlmon's character can be found in Glassco's *Memoirs of Montparnasse,* though Glassco met him too late to be truly impressed with him as a writer. Glassco describes the act which McAlmon, when especially drunk, used to put on in nightclubs:

> Bob downed half the fresh drink and stood up again. 'I'm going to sing! This is an aria from my Chinese opera.' He raised his arms, opened his mouth wide and began a hideous, wordless, toneless screaming. The effect was both absurd and painful; a dead silence fell over the room. Reeling against his stool, his head raised to the ceiling like dog, yowling, he suddenly seemed to be no longer a

drunken nuisance but a man who had gone mad; he was, I thought, actually either out of his mind or trying to become so. Suddenly he turned white, staggered, looked around wildly, and fell back into the arms of the big dinner-coated Negro who had appeared at the bar. (page 59)

The whole literary phenomenon of Paris in the 20's was ended by the Wall Street Crash and the Depression; its demise was signalled for many people by the strange suicide of Harry Crosby. Unlike many of his compatriots, however, McAlmon was unwilling to abandon Europe. Despite the fact that his money was running out, and that his literary career was no farther on than it had been in 1921, McAlmon spent the 30's in almost constant travel throughout Europe and America. He completed his autobiography, *Being Geniuses Together,* and after several attempts was able to get it published in London in 1938. It was either attacked or ignored. Joyce, by this time disenchanted with McAlmon, described it (very unfairly) as 'the office-boy's revenge.' (It was eventually republished, by Doubleday, in 1968, edited and with supplementary chapters by Kay Boyle.)

In the winter of 1939-40, McAlmon was living in France; he was forced to flee south to Lisbon, and from there, in the fall of 1940, he returned to America for the last time. His brothers gave him a job for the Southwest Surgical Supply Company, selling trusses and medical undergarments; he worked at this throughout the 40's, first in Phoenix and later in El Paso. During this time he was suffering from tuberculosis, and finally, in 1951, too sick to work anymore, he retired to Desert Hot Springs, California, where he spent his remaining years. Waiting for him when he arrived there was a copy of Williams' *Autobiography,* which shattered their relationship and left McAlmon in his final years embittered and separated from his closest friend. In the summer of 1952, he jouneyed east, and spent some time in New York. It was his last futile attempt to assert his literary position. By the end of the year, he was back in the desert for good.

Robert McAlmon died, of pneumonia, on the 2nd of February 1956, in Desert Hot Springs.

II

The relationship between the historical Robert McAlmon, whose biography is outlined above, and the Robert McAlmon who speaks in these poems is best described by Dorothy Livesay in her essay on the documentary poem in Canada, when she talks of 'a conscious attempt to create a dialectic between the objective facts and the subjective feelings of the poet.' It is hard, even for me, to disentangle what I know of McAlmon from what I have imagined about him.

Whenever possible, I have stuck close to the facts as I know them; but where it seemed necessary I have not hesitated to modify, rearrange, or even invent some incidents. But my inventions have been modest: the more bizarre the event (for example, the knife attack on Ezra Pound) the more likely it is to be accurate. Similarly, with McAlmon's character and opinions, I have usually started from what I know he thought and believed. But here, obviously, my own interpretations and creations are inescapable. From this point of view, it will be best if the reader accepts the McAlmon of these poems as a character in a historical fiction.

Few of McAlmon's own works are now in print, but the University of Southern Illinois in 1977 re-issued *A Hasty Bunch* in its 'Lost American Fiction' series. (It is to be hoped that someone will follow up by reprinting *Distinguished Air.*) Many of McAlmon's autobiographical stories are included in Robert E. Knoll's *McAlmon and the Lost Generation: A Self-Portrait* (University of Nebraska Press, 1962). The 1968 Doubleday edition of *Being Geniuses Together* is indispensable reading, all the more so for the double perspective provided by the Kay Boyle chapters. I have also made extensive use of Sanford J. Smoller's biography, *Adrift Among Geniuses* (Pennsylvania State University Press, 1975).

McAlmon appears as a character in most of the numerous volumes of 1920's autobiography. Out of this vast array I will mention only the two best, Gertrude Stein's *The Autobiography of Alice B. Toklas* (New York, 1933), and John Glassco's *Memoirs of Montparnasse* (Toronto: Oxford University Press, 1970). It was in this latter volume that I first came across the name of Robert McAlmon, and it is to John Glassco, in gratitude and deep admiration, that I address these poems.

Stephen Scobie,
Edmonton, Alberta,
1977.

93

McAlmon's Chinese Opera is a documentary fantasy about an American who didn't make it in the Paris of the 20's. Robert McAlmon knew everyone and was not without literary talent yet he wound up selling trusses in Arizona and died alone, abandoned by his friends and his dreams of success.

This poem-sequence reconstructs the life of McAlmon with consummate skill, particular upon particular, so that we witness not only the unfolding of an individual tragedy, but also new perspectives on a generation we have never been able to forget.

Stephen Scobie is a poet, critic, short-story writer, publisher and occasional journalist. His work has appeared in *Canadian Literature, Saturday Night* and *Weekend Magazine.* His works include *The Birken Tree* and a critical study, *Leonard Cohen.* He teaches at the University of Alberta where he is a founding editor of the literary press, Longspoon.